WHY PRAY?

WHY PRAY?
ROBERT LLEWELYN

Unpublished writings by the former chaplain
to the shrine of Julian of Norwich

Compiled and edited by
DENISE TREISSMAN

DARTON · LONGMAN + TODD

First published in 2019 by
Darton, Longman and Todd Ltd
1 Spencer Court
140–142 Wandsworth High Street
London SW18 4JJ

ISBN 978-0-232-53378-1

A catalogue record for this book is available from the British
Library.

Designed and produced by Judy Linard
Printed and bound in Great Britain by Bell & Bain, Glasgow

With gratitude and blessings to
Norfolk Emergency Services and
National Health Service,
without whom I would not be here
Denise Treissman

Contents

CONTENTS

Acknowledgements

My heartfelt gratitude goes to:
Robert Llewelyn and Geoffrey Treissman for teaching me the meaning of love, prayer and meditation.

Sr Christine at SLG Press for her encouragement and permission to use text from *Prayer and Contemplation* by Robert Llewelyn.

Jules Allen for her inspiration in the preparation of the images within the book.

Dori Veness for her technical help in putting Robert's work onto computer and together with Edward Jones and Sybil Jones for sharing spiritual inspiration and a love of silence.

Dr Rowan Williams for his encouragement and permission to use his words about Robert on the front cover.

Keith Rose for his advice and help with the manuscript.

Liz French for her friendship and advice about publishing.

Paul and Joan Golightly for providing a wonderful centre of prayer and spirituality that gave a quiet place of light for my work on this book.

Andrew Taylor and Margaret Taylor for their contribution to the book.

My family and friends for their love, encouragement and support.

Special thanks go to Sandy Mason, Cathy Russell, June and John Blythe for their help after Robert's death.

Christine Bromley and Tom Abbas for their beautiful words.

Judy Linard, David Moloney, Will Parkes, Helen Porter and the team at DLT for their help and support.

A BRIEF
INTRODUCTION TO
ROBERT LLEWELYN

Robert Llewelyn was Chaplain and a 'praying presence' in the cell of Mother Julian of Norwich from 1976 to 1990. He was known as a man of prayer, and was generous and enthusiastic about sharing his discoveries in prayer with others.

Before he died at the age of ninety-eight on February 6th, 2008 he had asked me to look after his affairs: it has been a joy to compile his unpublished work on prayer into this small book comprising of some of his talks, articles and leaflets, spanning five decades, but with an immediacy and universal appeal relevant to life today.

People came from around the world to see Robert, to enjoy his warm hospitality and love, to share silence with him, for spiritual direction, and to discuss their lives with him. Robert would always know the right book to give or lend, or would offer the appropriate leaflet to answer questions: he was encouraging and informative, always gentle, with a self-deprecating humour, and was known for his love of God, of people and of silence.

When Robert found a quote that helped him, he would type it out and print it and then stick it on his lounge door for everyone to see. Two memorable ones were: 'Silence is God's first language; everything else is a poor translation'[1] and, 'When two or more people share a profound silence, they bestow healing on one another'.[2]

Robert wrote many books on prayer, the first being *Prayer and Contemplation,* born out of his experience of living as a teacher, priest, Archdeacon and then Principal of Sherwood College in India, and later in 1972 living as part of the Anchorhold Community

---

[1] Fr Thomas Keating OCSO

[2] Donald Nicholl

in Haywards Heath, headed by Father Slade; one of its former residents called this community 'a laboratory of prayer'.

A former student of Robert's at Sherwood College said, in the film *Love was his Meaning*, made after Robert's death to celebrate his life and influence, 'Robert taught us love. As his students, we were all of different religions but under him we were one religion and that was love.' Also in that film, a friend who used to visit Robert for spiritual counsel said: 'Robert made you feel as if you were the most important person in the whole world: you felt treasured, loved, mothered.'

Robert visited places in France connected with the spiritual reading he had done and was to write later in his autobiography, *Memories and Reflections*, of the positive influences on him of Taizé, the Curé d'Ars, St Francis de Sales and Jean-Pierre de Caussade. One of St Francis's quotes he shares is: 'in the end only the language of the heart can reach another heart, while mere words as they slip from your tongue don't get past your listener's ear.'

This small book offers some of Robert's unpublished talks and writing on prayer and celebrates, as explained in a lovely way in Robert's philosophy of life on pages 13 – 16, the importance of prayer for life.

The book is divided into four sections: What Is Prayer?; Advice on Prayer from *Revelations of Divine Love* by the fourteenth-century mystic Lady Julian of Norwich; Ways of Praying; and The Fruits of Prayer.

The question, 'Why pray?' is answered clearly by Robert's words throughout the book in an encouraging way: as Lady Julian says, 'for it [prayer] does good'.

Denise Treissman
(Robert Llewelyn's Literary Executor)

MY PHILOSOPHY OF LIFE BY ROBERT LLEWELYN

For my philosophy of life I must begin with a story. I picture a village in India which has all it needs to maintain a simple social life; everything that is, except that it has no water. There is a large tank which the rain kept filled in better days and a distance away there is a well whose water can be used only by transferring it bucket by bucket. Every time a villager puts aside some personal inclination to make that trek across the fields they are pouring into that village the water of life. As the bucket is brought homewards its bearer can have no idea what this pail of water will do. Will it ease the last moments of a dying child, or fertilize a tiny piece of land, or be there for the washing of clothes or the scrubbing of a floor? Who can say? But the water is brought, immersed in the common pool of healing, and that is enough.

We live in a global village and all that we do is inter-related. Each one of us has the choice whether or not to bring the water of life into our stricken world. St Paul bids us to pray without ceasing and this is something to which we may all aspire, seeing prayer as the perpetual inclination of the heart towards God rather than the movement of the lips, though it is the second which will be needed to establish the first. Every prayer which passes my lips or carries the desire of my heart is, as it were, a bucket filled with the water of life. I have no idea what that prayer will accomplish, nor do I ask. It is enough that I put aside my natural sloth and with such love and devotion as is given me offer what I can to be joined with the aspirations of people of good will in every place. It is revealed to Julian that we are to pray wholeheartedly even though we find no joy in it, 'for it does good'. At the very least it does good to myself and that good cannot help affecting the next person I meet and so a chain reaction is set up. But it goes well beyond that. Somehow, somewhere, in answer to every prayer or praise uttered, or psalm recited or prayerful silence observed, with such sincerity as may be given us, good overcomes evil, light dispels darkness, truth supplants error and, if only in the minutest measure, the world is changed. So, too, for every stranger welcomed or loving deed performed.

On April 25th 2002 there died in Buenos Aires at the age of 102 a remarkable lady, Indian by name though European by birth. Indra Devi was still doing her yoga headstand in her late nineties. But more important was her philosophy of life. 'You give love and light to everyone, those who love you, those who harm you, those whom you know, those whom you don't know. It makes no difference. You just give light and love'. 'At eventide' says St John of the Cross, 'they will examine you in love', and he tells us that where there is no love we are to pour love in and we shall draw love out. No matter how far we fall behind the saints of every faith, the way is open for our sacrifice to be made in the knowledge that even a cup of water lovingly offered will not be despised. This I believe to be the only philosophy that can save us all.

From *Five Gold Rings*,
edited by Anna Jeffery
(Darton, Longman and Todd, 2003)

WHAT IS PRAYER?

Prayer is Waiting

I have been to Taizé only once and that was about 25 years ago. Frère Roger Schütz spoke to us on several occasions. I can remember just five words of what he said, and they have come back to me again and again. 'For me' , he said, 'prayer is waiting.'

There is much in Scripture to support those words. 'The Lord is good to those who wait for him', says Jeremiah. 'They that wait for the Lord shall renew their strength' writes Isaiah. 'I waited patiently for the Lord, and he heard my cry', from the Psalms. And more than two thousand years later, and moving beyond the Bible to St John of the Cross, we read that in prayer we are to learn to rest with attention in loving waiting upon God.

And so, when the time for silence comes, I ask you to take up your position for prayer (and sitting is usually best for most of us), and then, having asked the help of the Holy Spirit, to be content to wait, patiently, expectantly, lovingly, longingly. Try to realise this is all that you can do for yourself. God must do the rest. See yourself as the parched earth looking upwards waiting patiently for the rain to fall. You can neither hasten the shower nor determine its intensity when it comes. You can only wait.

We all need healing. We are all wounded souls. We are like Humpty Dumpty: we have had a great fall, but mercifully, unlike him, there is one who can put us together again. And that one, at this time of waiting, stands at your side. 'Rest in me', he says, 'and I in you.' See yourself as resting in Jesus as a child rests in its mother's arms. Allow him to bear you and enfold you in his love. See him standing there and calling your name: 'John, Margaret, I love you, and I have loved you always as if you were the only person in the whole world to love. And now I want to heal you. Let me do the work. Give all the strains and stresses over to me.' And then just wait. All you need is to desire God, to desire to pray, and then to wait. Have in your mind, if it helps, a short centring word or prayer which you can repeat silently as often as you need. Just the word 'Jesus', or the familiar 'Be still, and know that I am God' would do well. You may find it best to look mentally to the level of the heart.

It may not be long before distracting thoughts intrude. The rule here is that you may acknowledge them or recognise them, but you are not to develop them or encourage them, or in any way to get involved with them. Let them drop from your consciousness as a stone may drop into the sea. And if they won't drop away but insist on floating on the periphery of consciousness, then be content to let them float. But do not attempt to draw them in to yourself. These distractions may be due to external circumstances, such as a neighbour's radio, to which one may respond with forbearance or annoyance. If we choose the latter then an opportunity for growth in patience has been missed. Or they may have an interior cause. Anxieties, resentments, jealousies and the like may surface from the unconscious at such times that God's healing light may play upon them. This process is not without pain. In either case, if we respond with patience and perseverance, a dying to self and a rising to new life in Christ is taking place. Here is a part of the Holy Spirit's work of growth and sanctification.

This period of waiting is sure to be demanding. And you will find yourself asking: 'Is it any use? Am I really praying?' And here are words of comfort. And they come from St Augustine. 'Your very desire is itself your prayer; if your desire is continued so is your prayer also. Whatever you are doing, if you are desiring to pray, you are praying. If you do not wish to cease from prayer, do not cease from desire'. And these words are true, the intention or the desire **is** prayer whether we are speaking of vocal prayer, eucharistic prayer, office prayer, Jesus prayer, rosary prayer or, as now, the prayer of the silence of the heart before God.

If, then, you are tempted to ask whether you are really praying, all you have to do is ask yourself one question. Do I desire to pray? Am I desiring God? And if the answer is yes, then you are truly at prayer. Even if all you can do is to desire to desire to pray that is enough.

Now, this is very important. Sometimes people may speak as if correct posture is prayer. Sitting with a straight back assists prayer partly because it helps you to be attentive and alert, and partly because, it assists abdominal breathing. But correct posture in itself *is* not prayer. And correct breathing is not prayer. What then is prayer? It is the intention or desire to pray.

Or you may hear that relaxation is prayer. Relaxation assists prayer because it helps us to be receptive. But relaxation in itself is not prayer. Prayer is the intention or desire to pray.

Or some may speak as if bodily stillness

is prayer. Bodily stillness assists prayer because it helps to the stilling of the mind. But bodily stillness in itself is not prayer. Again, then, what is prayer? It is the intention or desire to pray.

Or not uncommonly today people may speak as if a change of consciousness is prayer. It may happen that in the silence we are taken from the ordinary workaday state of beta consciousness to that of alpha. This is a restful experience and where it is of the Holy Spirit it will be welcomed. But in itself an altered consciousness is not prayer. It can, for example, be induced by drugs or demonic forces; or simply by deep relaxation. What then is prayer? At the risk of being wearisome let it be said once more that it is the intention to pray, or the desire for God, which determines whether we are praying.

Undoubtedly in this period of waiting, waiting, we are sometimes taken hold of. The parched earth is rewarded with a shower of rain. St Antony the Great says that he prays best who does not know he is praying.

Watch a group of children at play. They are so engrossed in their game that they do not know they are playing. There is no corner in a child's mind which can allow him to say, 'Now, I am playing'. If, perchance, he does say that, then the game for him has at once lost some of its perfection. It is the same at prayer. Periods may pass when there is no corner of the mind which can say, 'Now, I am praying'. Just as you cannot say in bed at night, 'Now, I am sleeping', but can only say in the morning , 'I slept', so you cannot now say at prayer, 'Now, I am praying,' but can only say later, 'I prayed'. I am not speaking of any exalted state. If the phone rings you will hear it at once. These showers of rain, as it were, come and go, and the parched earth cannot determine their time or intensity. So, too, these periods of which I have spoken depend on God and not on us. They may be waited for, but not sought, least of all striven after: striving would in any case be in vain.

Prayer is waiting, intending, desiring God. Prayer, we might say, is a holding on

to God, until waiting, waiting, waiting, we
move into the knowledge that we are being
held.

Taken from a talk at a Taizé service at
Norwich Roman Catholic Cathedral on
24 November, 1995 (adapted)

Prayer is Offering

I think it helps if we can see prayer as an offering. If we are able to see prayer in this way, one important consequence will follow. We shall be relieved of all desire to make prayer successful, whatever that may mean. All sorts of thoughts may steal into our minds during prayer. Does this prayer help? Is it strengthening? Is it of any value for the person I am holding up before God? If we can see prayer as an offering we can ignore all these thoughts. A child doesn't make an offering to his mother that he may be helped or strengthened. The offering is simply to be offered as a token of love. Whether it helps or not is beside the point. So, too, if we can see prayer as an offering, we do not have to think about, much less be concerned about, what our prayer may achieve.

The offering of prayer may never be disengaged from the total offering of life. In so far as our working life is open to God to that extent will our prayer life be open, and in so far as our prayer life is exposed to the operation of the Spirit, to that extent will our working life be similarly exposed. Life is to be seen as a whole and it is only for the purpose of analysis that we may think of our prayer life separately. In the end the whole of life is to become prayer so that the distinction between work and prayer will become increasingly blurred. But in practice this can only happen if we are faithful and generous in our prayer life.

Jock Dalrymple in his book *The Christian Affirmation* has a telling phrase: 'You can only pray all of the time everywhere if you pray some of the time somewhere.' In Community you do a great deal of praying. In the world people constantly need their will stirred that they may keep their time of prayer. It's so easy to put off the prayer time, to discover so many things which need to be done when it comes round. But in Community there are the set times. The Rule takes care of this. But we still need the Spirit to stir our wills that we may be faithful and generous in these times. Monsignor Hughe in his book *Tension and Change* says that the capital sin against which we should be on our guard in the spiritual life is neither pride nor sensuality but sloth, that here is the main obstacle to prayer which is often arid, difficult and demanding of hard effort. It is here that the Spirit must first stir our wills. And yet that has to be done gently, sometimes almost imperceptibly. What is impetuous in our prayer life is not of the Spirit but of ourselves.

Part of the difficulty in silent prayer is its seeming futility. We appear to be wasting time. We seem to be doing nothing. Abbot Chapman, says in one of his letters that contemplative prayer often seems to be a pretty idiotic state. That is what our feelings are telling us. And what a fraud our feelings are! Yet how often do we not allow ourselves to be victimised by them? And when we think prayer is a waste of time and are tempted to give it up we must ask God to renew our faith. So far from it being a waste of time, it is the one time when we are up against the real enemy, 'face to face', it has been said, 'not with effects, not with symptoms, but with causes. The ultimate truth about things is not with things visible but in a cause which lies behind the visible.'

If you see someone floating in the water you may say that that person is doing nothing. He is simply resting on his back. Yet if he were to have a heart attack and die then he would truly do nothing and sink. And so against all appearances he was working hard before. He wasn't struggling. That is the mistake the beginner makes. If in learning to float any struggling is involved it is in struggling not to struggle, to give yourself over to the water, to let the water do its own work. So in prayer we have to learn to rest in the Spirit and to let the Spirit rest in us, to allow ourselves to be held by him. I do not mean by this we are to be inactive. I have just been re-reading that gem of a book *The Way of a Pilgrim*. The Jesus Prayer did not just go on of its own accord like a perpetual flame. One of our hermit sisters at Bede House gave me good advice about the Jesus Prayer: 'Support the Jesus Prayer until it supports you'. And I think that that advice holds for all prayer. We are to go on supporting it until it supports us.

I would like to end this reflection with the passage from St John of the Cross which comes from chapter ten of *The Dark Night of the Soul* and deals with perseverance in prayer:

> *The way they are to conduct themselves (in prayer) in this night of the sense is to devote themselves not at all to reasoning and meditation since this is not the time for it, but to allow the soul to remain in peace and quietness although it may seem clear to them that they are doing nothing and wasting their time, and although it may appear that it is because*

of their weakness that they have no desire in that state to think of anything. The truth is that they will be doing quite sufficient if they persevere in prayer, only leaving the soul free without making any effort [these last four words are in the original but not in the translation being now used] and disencumbered and at rest from all knowledge and thought, troubling not themselves in that state about what they shall think or meditate upon, but contenting themselves with a merely peaceful and loving attentiveness towards God, and in being without anxiety, without the ability, and without the desire to have experience of him or to perceive him. For all these yearnings disquiet and distract the soul from the peaceful, quiet and sweet sense of contemplation which is here granted to it. And although further scruples may come to them - that they are wasting their time and that it would be well for them to do something else, because they can neither do nor think anything in prayer — let them suffer these scruples and remain in peace.

Talk at St Mary and the Angels Convent,
Boxmoor on 25 November, 1973

Advice on Prayer from Lady Julian of Norwich

in *Revelations of Divine Love*

JULIAN'S ADVICE
ON PRAYER

I would like to share with you a few reflections on prayer based on Mother Julian's book *The Revelations of Divine Love*.

In chapter 41 of *Revelations*, which is the first of three consecutive chapters on prayer, Julian writes that prayer is 'the deliberate and persevering action of the soul'. That is to say, in our partially redeemed state in which the drawing of the spirit has to compete with the pulling of the flesh - interpreting flesh in the widest sense to include greed, envy, anger and the like - we do not fall into prayer effortlessly as we fall into sleep or the eating of our daily meals. Julian reminds us that prayer has to be worked at. It begins with a deliberate choice and it makes demands on our resolution as we proceed with it. Yet it will be our experience that as we grow in the grace of God, prayer becomes increasingly the natural desire of the heart. Our cry becomes one with St Augustine: 'You have made us for yourself and our heart is restless until it finds its rest in you'. Or with the writer of the 42nd Psalm: 'My soul thirsts for God, even for the living God, when shall I come to appear before the presence of God'. Such times will increase, says Julian, as the soul opens out to God. 'The nearer we are to our bliss', she writes, 'the more we shall long both by nature and grace.' 'And so it will continue', says Julian, 'until the day we die, still longing for love.' We may gratefully acknowledge that Julian's experience is, in some measure, coming to be our own. Yet we shall be wise not to forget her words that prayer is a deliberate choice calling for resolution and perseverance.

Probably most of us can look back to a time when we went to prayer only when a crisis arose or some disaster threatened. I am reminded of the sailor who, when asked by Dr Johnson if he had had a good voyage, replied that it had been first rate adding for good measure, 'in fact we only had to turn to prayer twice and once it was hardly necessary'. Although we shall hopefully have advanced beyond that point we shall still find within us a mixture of motives when we turn to prayer. This need be no cause for anxiety for it is prayer itself which purges these motives of their lower element. At every point God accepts us as we are and looks upon us as, through his grace, we are coming to be. To turn to God because our souls are in a state of unrest crying out for the consolation of this presence is not something deserving of reproach. On the contrary we should welcome this incentive to pray. 'When a soul is tempted and troubled and left to herself in her unrest,' writes Julian 'then is the time to pray so as to make the soul more responsive and obedient towards God.' 'But', she adds significantly, 'No kind of prayer can make God more responsive to the soul, for God is always constant in love'. The change must always be on our part. It cannot, in the nature of things be on God's, because his love is constant, steady and unchangeable, always directed unswervingly towards our needs. To turn to prayer is to expose ourselves to God so that we may be able to receive what he is always anxious and ready to give.

Yet. Notwithstanding what has been said, we are always to be moving towards the point whereby we go to God for his sake and not our own. We are to be people who search for God for what he is and not for what we get from him. As our motives are purified, that is to say as they are increasingly governed by God's love, we shall in fact find that same love more richly shed abroad in our hearts. It is a truth of prayer that the less self-regarding it becomes the more self-rewarding it will be. Archbishop William Temple has made a parallel remark in regard to intercession. 'Prayer which is mainly occupied with a result to be obtained is comparatively powerless to obtain results."

The priest together with members of religious communities have a great advantage over the ordinary person in the quest of God for his own sake in that they are bound by the saying of the daily office. Thus, independently of feeling or convenience, they are under obedience propelled towards God at set times of the day sometimes when their hearts are crying out for the consolation of prayer, at other times when they are dry and cold and would gladly seek solace in other directions. The obligation and objectivity of the office are its great strengths, rescuing us from being victims of our preference and our moods, mortifying our wills, as the old phraseology has it, and setting before us God's eternal truths as expressed in lesson and psalm and prayer. It is faithfulness to some rule governing our prayer life which makes God our rock and strength and which prevents us from becoming butterfly creatures, finding life in its shallows rather than in its depths. In exercising such discipline we are but doing in our own lives what we expect every housewife to do in hers. The wife and mother who cooks for the young family only when the mood is on her and when she feels the inclination to do so, is not the sort of person on whom anyone would depend. It is faithfulness to the task to be done in times good and bad which makes for the building of character.

Julian gives forcible expression to our thinking at this point in one of her best-known passages on prayer. In chapter 41 drawing on her fourteenth Revelation she writes: 'He says (we note these introductory words for they mean that the teaching is not Julian's but is that given her by God) "Pray wholeheartedly, even though you find no joy in it. For it does good though you feel nothing, see nothing, even though you think you cannot pray. For when you are dry and empty, sick and weak, your prayer is pleasing to me, even though there is little enough to please you. All believing prayer is pleasing in my sight.' The direct communication ends at this point and

Julian's comment follows. God, she tells us wants us to pray and accepts our work and goodwill no matter how we feel.

'Pray wholeheartedly.' The Middle English word here is *inerdly* and there is some dispute as to whether that translates as *wholeheartedly* or *inwardly*. Colledge and Walsh favour the former, others the latter. If Julian could be consulted I feel sure she would say that we do well to accept both translations. Praying wholeheartedly means that the full energies of the soul are to be engaged in prayer whether it be expressed vocally or interiorly. 'Pray inwardly' speaks especially of the interior silence of the heart before God. Whilst we may believe that most of Julian's own prayer time was passed in contemplative silence, we must note that vocal petitionary prayer has prominence in her book. Nowhere does she suggest, as one finds is sometimes assumed, that vocal prayer is a suitable exercise for beginners that may be expected to be outgrown in later life. Nor does she downgrade, much less despise, the petitionary aspect of prayer though she sets it in the context of adoration and directs it away from selfish desires. She is well aware that God is already on the scene before ever we come to pray and he wishes us to cooperate with him in the work he has in hand. *'He beholds us in love,'* she writes, *'and wants to make us partners in his goodwill and work.'* In that way we are drawn to God and come to see him as the source of all good. Whilst we may place all our needs before God as children before a loving father, we shall not be so naïve as to suppose that all our desires will coincide with God's will. Often, says Julian, we must be prepared to wait for further grace, or another time, or a better gift. Yet there are some petitions we can always make with confident trust. Thus we can always pray for mercy and grace or for a deepening knowledge of God's love. Julian's own great prayer, the ultimate we might say in the realm of petition, was 'God of your goodness give me yourself, for only in you I have all.'

Julian tells us very little of her own way of prayer. But she would no doubt have been acquainted with *The Ancrene Rule*, a rule for anchorites drawn up by Richard Poore, Bishop of Salisbury, about a hundred years before her time. These were times when the anchorite life flourished in England and *The Ancrene Rule* had a considerable influence upon it. It offered guidance to every aspect of the anchorite's life and as we would expect, instruction on prayer, its form and frequency, held a prominent place. It is reasonable to assume Julian would have been influenced by this. On rising in the morning, after a few introductory prayers the rule bids the anchorite to say: 'Jesus Christ, son of the living God, have mercy on us! Thou who didst condescend to be born of a virgin have mercy on us!' The words were to be said repeatedly until the anchorite was dressed. But more than that, they are commended as words to which the heart may return and find its rest in God in every period of the day.

'Have these words in much use, says the rule, and in your mouth as often as ye may, sitting and standing.' I find it interesting to note the similarity of this prayer with the Jesus Prayer of the Orthodox Church which in its full form runs, 'Jesus Christ, son of the living God, have mercy on me a sinner.' And it will be noted that like the Jesus prayer the anchorite prayer is to be repeated over and over again. I think we may also assume that Julian used the rosary though doubtless in some less stylised form than is customary today. Certainly *The Ancrene Rule* bids the solitary to say the Hail Mary 'fifty or a hundred times, more or less as ye have leisure' and later we read 'I pray you that you never be idle but work or read, or *be at beads*, and in prayer, and this always be doing something from which good may come.' Julian herself gives evidence in chapter 19 of the Shorter Text of the prayers of the rosary writing, 'We say the Our Father, Hail Mary, I believe, with such devotions as God will give us.'

Thus it seems to me important teaching

for all of us here. Julian writes that prayer unites the soul to God making it one with his will through the deep inward working of the Holy Spirit. Repetitive prayer may be a powerful means of bringing that about. Paul bids us to pray without ceasing. We cannot interpret that as a call to unceasing formal prayer. Rather we are to understand that the heart is to be always at prayer - an activity which may continue unconsciously through the occupations of our working lives. But the flame in the heart will die unless it is frequently rekindled by conscious application. It is here that repetitive prayer has its part to play. The one who carries in the mind some short form of prayer will find countless opportunities for its use, and every usage will help to lodge it more deeply in the heart, so that instead of being a pray-er you become a prayer. Prayer is a holding on to God until one moves into the knowledge that one is being held.

Julian is very fond of words that express this holding on to God, words like clinging and cleaving. Thus she writes 'Our lover desires that our soul should cling to him with all its might, and that we should ever hold fast to his goodness For this above all pleases God and strengthens the soul'. Or again 'Cling to him and we shall be safe and sound from all kinds of danger.' Or yet again, 'When a soul holds on to God in trust whether in seeking him or contemplating him, this is the highest worship it can bring.'

We have therefore to be active in our seeking, to summon up the energies of our soul in our search for God.' This seeking, she tells us, pursued in the spirit of faith, hope and love, pleases God, and it leads on to a finding which 'pleases the soul, and fills it with joy'. 'It is God's will that we seek on until we see him, for it is through this that he will show himself to us, of his special grace, when it is his will.' Our seeking will be rewarded in beholding, and then it is that 'we have what we desire and do not see what more we should pray for but all our intention and all our prayer are wholly directed to contemplating him.' This she describes as 'an exalted and imperceptible prayer'. It is then 'that we can do no more than contemplate him and rejoice, with a great and compelling desire to be wholly united into him, and attend to his motion and rejoice in his love and delight in his goodness.'

A talk to the Society of the
Precious Blood in Peterborough

WAYS OF
PRAYING

SILENT PRAYER

Before you begin you may like to reflect:
This is my love-offering, aided by grace, sitting quietly in the presence of God, allowing all thoughts, memories and imaginations to drop away, knowing that God will use this offering for the extension of his kingdom.

Prayer is best seen as an offering to God that he may use it as he will. Through silent prayer we become more deeply rooted in Christ and so more effective instruments of God's grace. The effect of contemplative prayer, as seen by St John of the Cross, is to 'set the soul on fire with the spirit of love'. Love is the great healer and, firmly planted within, may well remove blockages in mind and body which no medicine or treatment can touch. We have it from St John the apostle, for example, that love is victorious over fear (1 John 4:18) which is so often at the root of mental and physical sickness. But to make the undoubted healing power of prayer more than a secondary motive for its practice tends to fix us upon ourselves rather than on God. We do better to direct our attention towards God, and to allow the rest to take care of itself.

The more we think of prayer as an offering to God, or better still as a love-offering, the less we shall be disturbed by doubts as to whether it is 'doing any good'. Offerings don't have to succeed: they simply have to be offered, and in such simplicity of heart as God may grant. When the going is hard it may help to reflect that you are there for God's sake and not your own. Consider, too, that you do not wish to make an offering which costs you nothing.

The test of prayer is its fruit. St Paul lists the fruits of the Spirit as: love, joy, peace, patience, kindness, goodness, faithfulness, gentleness, self-control. (Galatians 5: 22-23)

You may like to just sit quietly waiting upon God, or to use silently some form of words as: 'He enfolds us for love and will never let us go', or 'Be still and know that I am God', or words of your choice.

GOING DEEPER

This Ash Wednesday morning I found myself sitting next to a two-year-old child whose grandmother had brought her to church. She sat silently for a short while and then climbed on to granny's lap and remained contentedly in her arms for the full forty minutes. What was little Daisy doing? Seemingly nothing, but that is not correct. Unknowingly she was offering herself to be loved. The thought takes us to the deepest offering we can make in prayer, the offering of ourselves to God to be loved. We ourselves do nothing except that we make the offering and continue to make it (not thinking about it unless it be at the start and thereafter now and again) until the time is up, and we leave the work to be done by God. God loves us and enjoys us, as Julian of Norwich reminds us, but so often our 'busyness' and neglect prevent that love reaching us as he would wish. Here in the silence we are giving him the opportunity he longs for. And just as Daisy's love for her granny was further drawn out by granny's love for her, so our own love for God grows as a spontaneous (almost reflex) response to God's love for us. And the overspill of that love is, of course, found in our love for one another in daily life.

This thought can be a most encouraging one in our prayers. So often it seems that we are doing nothing and that it is just a waste of time, but so long as the offering remains, so does the prayer and we are fed by it more than we know. One of the rules of prayer is that it is not to be judged by how it feels at the time but (if judged at all) by its later fruit.

'Julian Meetings', which exist to encourage contemplative prayer in the Christian tradition, issue a prayer card which emphasises this deeper way of prayer. It deserves to be quoted in full.

> Relax your body
> and quieten your mind.
> Be open to God in the silence.
> God is with you – here – now.
> Do not strive or be anxious.
> Be silent, be still
> and let God reach you.
> Let God love you.

Some Thoughts on Silent Prayer
(2004)

Prayer as Praise

About fifteen years ago when I was going through a difficult patch in my life I was asked to drive Fr Christopher Bryant of the Cowley Fathers from somewhere in Essex to the mother house in Oxford. It was a journey of several hours and I took the opportunity of opening out to him, for he was, as any of you who knew him well will know, skilled in spiritual direction. After I had finished he said less than a dozen words. 'Have you tried thanking God for everything? And then he added, 'And I mean *everything*', placing an emphasis on the last word. I won't say it was a new thought, for the Bible and especially the psalms are plentiful in commending praise and thanksgiving. But it came to me that afternoon in a new way and I began to realise how little I had entered into the spirit of what the Bible and the church, especially through the Eucharist, which word means thanksgiving, had been proclaiming to me all my life. From then on, I have sought God's grace to follow that advice. Sometimes it has been hard and I have been wanting in faith or courage. But through it all the desire has persisted and it is on this subject, praise and thanksgiving, that I want to turn to now.

If I were speaking to beginners, and I know I am speaking to seasoned warriors rather than raw recruits (though by a strange paradox that makes it more likely that you consider yourself to be a beginner), my advice would be to begin this matter of praise with what comes easily and naturally, often spontaneously, thanking and praising God for good friends, good health, and for all the good things which bring pleasure, beautiful scenery, inspiring music and so on.

Some years ago I was sent a blessing poem and asked to use it as I liked. I thought it beautiful and I will share it with you here.

Lord of all Blessing
As we walk about your world

Let us know ourselves blessed at every
     turn;
Blessed in the autumnal sun and leaves;
Blessed in the winter wind;
Blessed in rain and shafts of sunlight;
Blessed in the moving of stars;
Blessed in the turning of the world
     beneath our feet;
Blessed in silence;
Blessed in sleep;
Blessed in our children, our parents
     and our friends;
Blessed in conversation and the human
     voice;
Blessed in waiting for the bus or train
     or traffic lights;
Blessed in music, blessed in singing
     voices, blessed in the song of birds;
Blessed in the cry that pierces the heart;
Blessed in the smile of strangers;
Blessed in the touch of love, blessed in
     laughter;
Blessed in pain, in darkness, in grief;
Blessed in the desert and the frost;
Blessed in waiting for Spring;

Blessed in waiting and waiting and
    waiting.
Lord of all blessing, we bless you.

(Hugh Dickinson, Dean of Salisbury)

For the most part those graceful words speak of the pleasing things of life, though near the end there comes a break with the line: 'Blessed in pain, in darkness and in grief.' We should certainly praise God for 'the autumnal sun and leaves', but if our praise remains at that level we are still what St Paul calls 'babes in Christ', and have not learnt how to digest the strong meat which Paul calls us to do. So let me take another quotation, this time from the seventeenth-century writer, William Law, which balances the passage I have read. This, you will note, is somewhat severe, and brooks no nonsense. But it is a powerful piece of writing:

As thankfulness is an express acknowledgement of the goodness of

God towards you, so repinings and complaints are as plain accusations of God's want of goodness towards you.

If anyone would tell you the shortest, surest way to all happiness and perfection, he must tell you to make it a rule for yourself to thank and praise God for everything that happens to you. For it is certain that whatever seeming calamity happens to you, if you thank and praise God for it you turn it into a blessing. Could you therefore work miracles, you could not do more for yourself than by this thankful spirit, for it turns..... all that it touches into happiness.

It is a powerful quotation and yet I think there is a weakness in Law's last sentence for it suggests that happiness is the object or reason for praise and thanksgiving thus bringing the mind back to fasten on itself. The purpose of praise is quite simply to give God his due. Happiness will follow but the less we think about it the better. Or more simply, happiness is the result of praise (perhaps I should say long term result), but it is not the motivation for it.

Praising God in 'pain, darkness and grief' (to return to my first quotation) is not an easy thing to do. This might almost be the understatement of the year. Praising God in pain and darkness and grief is (if I may use a powerful metaphor which is not my own) like trying to push a car with the brakes on. It is always pleasant to the natural man or woman within us when in the time of praise the emotions go along with the will. But often they do not. They are frequently cold or they may be in rebellion. However, if you try pushing cars with the brakes on, although you may not get very far, you will if you persevere, have done wonders for your own muscles and it will seem relatively easy to push them when the brakes are taken off and they are allowed to run freely. And it is the same with praise. If we build up the habit of praising God in the adverse circumstances of life we shall find ourselves living in the spirit of praise and thanksgiving, something which Meister Eckhart calls the mark above all which characterises a truly Christian life.

George Herbert expresses our thought eloquently:

> Thou who hast given so much to me,
> Give one thing more, a grateful heart.
> Not thankful when it pleases me,
> As though thy blessing had spare days;
> But such a heart whose pulse may be,
> Thy praise.

From a talk given to Kaleidoscope,
Norwich 1999

The Sacrifice
of Praise

'We do not praise God because he has caused us to, but because to praise God *is* to triumph.' I suppose most people have a saying which they carry with them over a period of life and I gladly share mine with the reader. I came across it perhaps twelve years ago in a collection of sayings of Richard Benson, founder of the Cowley Fathers. Through it a new light is thrown on our customary conceptions of success and failure. There is, it says, only one failure and that is to be found not in the situation itself, afflictive though it may be, but in allowing the situation to drive you to bitterness and regret, to despondency and despair. The antidote is praise, praise and thanksgiving, whatever the circumstances. I shall use here the word 'blessing' to hold the two together.

The saying is not surprisingly matched by St Paul. 'In everything give thanks.' I note that the preposition is 'in' not 'for' and I have often wondered if we may press the difference. If adversity overtakes me, does Paul mean that I should bless God *in* the situation but not necessarily *for* it? If, for example, I am unjustly sent to prison it accords with reason that I should praise God *in* my new environment. It would be an odd sort of Christian who now ceased to attend the Eucharist simply because the prison chapel and not the parish church was open to him. But to be told that I should bless God *for* the injustice done to me strains not only faith but reason, for it may appear that I am thus being asked to pronounce evil as praiseworthy which is manifestly absurd.

And yet I think that for Paul it would have been both 'in' and 'for' and that ultimately the distinction is apparent rather than real. Paul would have blessed God in prison because it was his habit to bless God continually, and he would have blessed

God for prison because he would have been assured in the power of faith that God was planning to use the injustice for his greater glory, both within Paul himself (which he would probably scarcely have thought of), and in the world around. Thus Paul's imprisonment in Philippi ended with the conversion of the jailer and the baptism of himself with his family.

How then stands our philosophical objection? There is none (given Paul's view of God's providential ordering of the world) so long as we realise that it is not evil itself which is praiseworthy, but that what is praiseworthy is that God should allow this particular evil to take place. God is being praised not for the evil but for his wisdom, forbearance and foresight in permitting it, and thus continuing to honour his gift of free will to humankind. Paul would have seen everything to be in God's hands and that nothing could take place except under his sufferance. He would have been at one with St Augustine who wrote that God can permit evil only in so far as he is capable of turning it into good. At this point we can hardly fail to recall Paul's own words: 'We know that in everything God works for good in those who love him, who are called according to his purpose.' (Romans 6:26)

'In everything give thanks.' Paul who had suffered so greatly must have been fully aware of the demanding nature of his charge. It must surely be the most difficult of all the apostolic biddings to fulfil. I have written elsewhere that probably only a saint should make such a demand and certainly only a saint could fulfil it. None the less the precept remains to challenge us. What is important is that we should not shrink from it because we fear we can only respond at the lower levels. Knowing our insufficiency for the Himalayan heights (though it may be that for some a surprise is in store) we are not to fight shy of some robust exercise in the plains. Probably most mountaineers begin with clambering over the tool shed or shinning up a tree in the garden.

A heart alive in the spirit of praise and thanksgiving is perhaps the surest mark of a Christian life. 'If anyone would tell you the shortest, surest way to all happiness and perfection', writes William Law, 'he must tell you to make a rule to thank and praise God for everything that happens to you. Whatever seeming calamity happens to you, if you thank and praise God for it, you turn it into a blessing. Could you therefore work miracles you could not do more for yourself than by this thankful spirit, it turns all that it touches into happiness.' But to bless God continually is not a natural response, least of all when the circumstances are uncongenial.

To such moments we may apply the familiar Eucharistic phrase 'the sacrifice of praise and thanksgiving'. The word sacrifice signifies an offering and a costly offering at that. In the face of adversity the offering to begin in faith through the operation of the will. At this point it is not likely that the feelings will be on our side. The overflowing heart belongs to a later stage and must be waited for and allowed to come in its own time.

In her brief treatment of thanksgiving (though her whole book is a hymn of rejoicing in God) Julian of Norwich considers praise as gathering momentum within and then, as a river bursting its banks (my image not hers), sees it overflow into ecstatic words of delight: 'Good Lord, I thank you, blessed be your name.' (chapter 41) Julian expects her even-Christians to know such times and doubtless we have all experienced them. But she is too realistic to leave it there and writing as always from experience she continues: 'Sometimes when our hearts are dry and without feeling, or when we are assaulted by temptation, then we are driven by reason and grace to call upon our Lord, rehearsing his blessed passion and great goodness.' It is thus that the sacrifice of praise and thanksgiving finds its fulfilment, for left to our natural inclinations we would not be engaged in blessing God at such times.

Julian is beckoning us to allow the heart to be established in praise and thanksgiving through repeated acts of blessing. The Eucharist and Daily Office, arrow prayers from the heart, repetitive prayers offered in the spirit of thankfulness (hence Julian's "Prayer and thanksgiving belong together") such as the Our Father, the Hail Mary or the Jesus Prayer, together with those of our choice taken perhaps from the psalms, are all means whereby the heart may learn to beat in the joy and stillness of God. Prayer is thus carried over into periods when we cannot be consciously engaged in it. There will be occasions each day when a new impulse needs to be given, not simply at the regular set times, but sometimes at odd moments, the halt at traffic lights, the queue in the shop, the walk down the familiar street. Such periods will alternate with those in which the heart is simply to rest in the silence of God. In some such ways we are enabled to grow into becoming a focus of blessing which cannot but shed its portion of light on the world around us.

Acts of praise in the power of faith when the spirit is dulled and the heart is low have upon us a similar effect as the sun on mist at the start of a new Spring day. For a while it may seem that nothing is happening, but unseen the sun is working and by mid-day the haze is gone and we can bask in the warmth that embraces us. So too in the continual blessing of God comes the dispersal of our fears, our restlessness, our gloom on some days it may be, our heaviness of soul. 'Why art thou so heavy ... so disquieted ... put your trust in God ... I will yet give him thanks.' (Psalm 43).

Article in *Christian*
(1989)

The Rosary

INTRODUCTION

The rosary, in something like its present form, has been in use in the Western Church for almost a thousand years, and a custom which has so universally stood the test of the centuries should not lightly be discarded. The prayers and structure of the rosary are unique to the Christian Church, but the principle is common, if not universal, beyond the Christian faith, Our awareness of this should serve to enhance its value.

The rosary has been, for many, a way in to silent prayer. The silence of the heart before God is of the essence of the prayer life.

The rosary is 'a little way', asking of us no more than the simplicity of children, but to those practised in it it offers a rich reward. This, however, may never be seen as an individual possession for it is of the very nature of love to radiate light and peace and joy and to spend itself quietly in helpful and practical ways. It is thus that the life of society is transformed, the leavening of the lump from within working what no government fiat could ever achieve. And so it must be that the witness of the Church will always be to the priority of prayer if its influence is to make impact on society as a whole.

From *A Doorway to Silence –*
The Contemplative Use of the Rosary
(Darton, Longman and Todd, 1986)

HOW ROBERT FOUND THE ROSARY

I have found the rosary to be a heaven-sent blessing, especially where I can say it with others, devoting perhaps twenty minutes to its use and then fifteen minutes to the silence before God to which it leads.

It was in 1975 that I discovered the rosary. In August 1975 I spent several weeks in Ibiza (with friends). We used to go to evening mass at the church serving a small fishing port. We would arrive perhaps ten minutes before the service to find the men on one side and the women on the other reciting the rosary, each side answering the other. A deep reverence prevailed in that simple peasant church and the mass that followed was a contemplative experience for most of us. It was that that drew me to the rosary and later I was instructed in its use.

Let me begin by saying that there is only one way in which we can pray and that is to pray with the heart. By the heart I mean the innermost core of the personality. Call it the will or the desire if you like. The lips, the eyes and the ears, the nose and the touch, may be a great help to prayer, because and only because, they help to move the heart. The rosary is a means by which the lips and the touch and the ears (when in a group), and in varying degrees, the imagination (as in meditating on the mysteries) are used to move the heart to prayer.

Once on the radio, I said that you can say the rosary, if you wished, with your feet, and I went on to explain what I meant. Unfortunately the editor cut out the last bit and left listeners wondering how they could manipulate rosary beads on their toes. I was thinking, as I explained, of a Catholic priest who had come to see me, who said he had been praying an abridged rosary with his feet from the railway station to the Julian Cell. In each set of eight paces he said, Ho-ly Jes-us, Ho-ly Ma-ry. As he put down each foot, saying in his mind the corresponding syllable, he was uniting his heart again to God, living in a succession of present moments. That is a very good way of saying the rosary, or for that matter of using many other prayers. If the heart is moved to prayer that is all that matters. It is an exercise in celebrating the sacrament of the present moment, a phrase which was, so far as I know, first used by Jean-Pierre de Caussade.

From *Memories and Reflections*
(Darton, Longman and Todd, 1998)

The Rosary – A Help in Depression

Recently someone suffering from depression came to see me. I advised him to say the rosary using a short prayer in place of the Hail Mary, with which he would not have been familiar, on each decade bead. After we had looked at some possibilities together he chose 'The joy of the Lord is your strength' (Nehemiah 8:10). It may or may not shorten the depression. But it will make it easier to bear and help turn it to creative account.

But what is the rosary? Basically it is a circlet of fifty-five beads, counting a small medallion as one bead. To the medallion is also attached a short string of five beads (known as the pendant), ending with a cross or crucifix on which the rosary is normally begun with the recitation of a creed. Fifty of the circlet beads are arranged in groups of ten known as decades. Each decade is separated from the next by a 'spaced' bead. I advised my visitor to begin with an Our Father on the medallion and then to say the chosen prayer on each decade bead, allowing his mind to be gently (repeat gently) enfolded in the words. The words were to be allowed to dissolve in the heart, as a sweet might dissolve in the mouth. On the spaced bead between each decade he would say a Gloria. He could say the whole aloud (which would probably be best at first), or in a whisper, or silently with the lips closed and the tongue still. He was to do whichever was most natural, and not to strain after attention or devotion – but very simply to offer his prayer with such faith, love and devotion as might be given him.

VAIN REPETITION?

But someone may say that this is vain repetition. Repetition certainly, but not all repetition is vain. Hammer a nail into a wall, and you have repetition; but the repetition is not vain if the nail moves even slightly with each blow. And the repetition of the prayer is not vain if each recitation takes you a little more closely into the heart of God. You will soon know that things are very different on the fortieth bead from what they were on the first.

MERELY MECHANICAL?

Perhaps another objector will say that this is to make prayer merely mechanical. Mechanical, yes, but not merely so. Walking is mechanical, but it is not merely mechanical. You walk as a person, not as a zombie. Because you have mastered the mechanics of walking, you are free to talk to your companion. The mechanical element of the rosary sets the mind free to rest in God. Grasp this, and in understanding you have arrived. Repetitive prayer works first at the relatively superficial level in holding before the mind material for meditative reflection. Later (and much more importantly) it frees the mind for engagement at a deeper (subliminal) level. Thus the emerging, unfolding and deeper self is encountered and new energies of the Spirit are released.

FIVE GOOD REASONS

But why use the beads at all? Why not just recite the prayer? I have to speak from experience. I have done it that way most of my life, but I have found it a tremendous help to use the rosary itself. I think there are five reasons: 1. The rosary breaks up the time into small elements, and these can be dealt with one by one. 2. The pressure of the fingers on each successive bead is an aid to keep the mind from wandering. 3. The breaking up into five decades relieves the monotony of the exercise. 4. The audible repetition of the words helps to gather the attention into what is being done (though later you may like to use the rosary in silence). 5. The beads that remain to be worked are an encouragement to continue to the end.

THE MYSTERIES

Traditionally associated with the rosary are fifteen mysteries on one or other of which the user meditates according to the decade being said. These are beyond the scope of a brief article, but any booklet on the rosary will enlighten the reader. The almost effortless recitation of the prayer sets the mind free to dwell on the mystery (relating to some aspect of the life of Jesus or Mary) under consideration. At a certain stage, however, one may find that the mysteries hinder rather than help, the simple recitation of the prayer now acting as a magnet drawing one into contemplative silence. To attend to the things of God is good, but to attend to God himself is better. We shall soon discover that the quality of the silence now open to us is very different from what it was before the rosary was begun. Contemplation takes us into the very heart of the communion of saints. Meditation is a preliminary stage, preparing us for the deeper relationship God has in store.

DYING AND RISING IN CHRIST

A word of advice. The rosary is best said regularly as a discipline, and not just picked up when one feels in the mood to do so. Prayer belongs primarily to the will, and not the feelings. If the feelings are on our side, so be it. But, if not, they should simply be ignored. The rosary (and the silence beyond) is a purgation; and this in turn leads to a deepening union. Through it we are purified to the roots. Each bead is a dying, and with each death is a new rising in Christ. Thus by many deaths, we are prepared for that which is final.

AN ENRICHMENT FOR CHURCH AND NATION

The lives of many stand to be immeasurably enriched by the regular practice of the rosary. But the benefit will be for the whole Body of Christ. If tens of thousands of people were to say the rosary daily with such love and devotion as was given them (God asks no more), a new surge of spiritual life would be released, carrying with it an incalculable effect on Church and nation.

From *The Rosary as an Aid to Prayer*,
a leaflet reprinted and expanded from
an article in the *Church Times*

REFLECTIONS OF THE ROSARY

Wherever Mary appears – as at Lourdes, Fatima and now Medjugorje – she sees the rosary as a healing prayer for all and asks insistently for it. It is a remarkable prayer for it meets our need at all stages. If we are in the way of discursive meditation the rosary meets us as we let our minds dwell on the mystery we are passing through. If our stage is that of affective prayer, the mysteries will be largely left behind as we allow the words to draw us, bead by bead, into the silence of the heart before God. If we are on the fringe of contemplation the words themselves may for a while lose their meaning as we are taken into communion with God at a deeper level. Meditation (the first stage) is an attention to the things of God, whereas contemplation is attention to

God himself. Finally we shall want to lay the rosary aside and allow the Holy Spirit in silence to continue his healing work.

Newcomers to the rosary are liable to have three main difficulties.

- May one pray to Mary? Most of the Church says yes, but if anyone after reflection continues to think differently the traditional rosary is not for them. But not all is lost. See the rosary as a piano and the Hail Mary as a tune. A piano takes many tunes and you can choose your own for the rosary keeping to the traditional structure. You might use a simple affirmation on each decade bead: 'He enfolds us for love and will never let us go' (Julian of Norwich).

- Saying the Hail Mary fifty times is surely vain repetition? Repetition yes but not all repetition is vain. Our steps to church were repetition but each was made from a separate point to the one before and finally they took us to the altar of God. So, too, each bead takes us closer to the heart of God.

- 'Does it not make prayer merely mechanical?' Mechanical yes but not merely so. The mechanical element sets the mind free from attending to surface distractions, or enables it to meditate on the mysteries. Rosary users don't apologise for the mechanical element. They welcome it.

'Holy Mary … pray for us sinners, now, and at the hour of our death.' It is a prayer which heals our wounded natures, cutting through condescension and patronage – always a lurking peril in intercession – as we own ourselves to be at the same level of dependence and need as those for whom we pray.

From the leaflet
Reflections of the Rosary

Praying for Ourselves and Others

What should we ask for when we pray?

Below the intercession board in St Julian's Church, Norwich, where visitors leave their requests for prayer, we have written the following words:

> God in his wisdom has linked some of his blessings, we do not know in what manner or measure, to our patience and confidence in asking for them … Ask and you shall receive. God does not want us to puzzle our heads about the machinery of it all, he wants us to go to him like children, not ashamed to tell him what we have set our hearts on. Only, at the back of it all, the object of

prayer is not to make God want what we want, it is to make us want what God wants ... in his will lies our peace.

HIGHEST

So wrote Ronald Knox, and his words are a reminder that we may never lose sight of the petitionary aspect of prayer. Yet, is it right that we should ask for specific things? 'Surely not,' some will say; 'How can I presume to know what is best? I dare not do more than pray, "Thy will be done".'

I am often suspicious of that. Certainly I believe 'Thy will be done' is the highest expression of petitionary prayer. But I believe too that it may well be the lowest.

How glibly may the words slip off our lips in relation to someone who is ill or in trouble! It may be we never give a thought to the matter again. Although the prayer is part of the 'Our Father' I do not believe God always asks it of us.

Jesus did not despise the urgent request, the cry of the centurion, 'Lord, come down ere my child will die.' We all need to make this prayer at times, a prayer wrung from the heart by anguish and sorrow. Yet it is not the end of the way. I remember a woman, whose husband was dying of cancer, coming to me again and again urging me to pray for his recovery.

Then, one day, after about nine months, she came quietly and said: 'It's all right; he's in God's hands. He knows best. May his will be done.' That was progress, and victory, victory won in the crucible of suffering.

And so, when people say to me they can pray only that God's will be done, I often want to ask, if when your own dear child or husband (or it may be yourself) is at the gate of death, you can say quite simply (as did Martha and Mary) 'Lord, he whom thou lovest is sick,' commending your loved one with all your heart into God's care for what he sees best, then all is well, let this be your constant prayer. But, if not, look well again lest your prayer be shallow and superficial, and perhaps dangerous, for it may be an agent of self-deception.

OUR PEACE

'God appointed prayer,' wrote Father Benson, 'not because he had any formal delight in our homage, but by forming in us the habit of prayer to draw us to look to himself as the fountain of all good.'

Let us then not be too superior or ashamed to take to God the hopes and desires of our hearts. Only 'at the back of it all is the desire that we shall be brought to want what God wants, not that He shall want what we want...in His will lies our peace.'

And not ours only, but the peace of the one for whom we pray.

Eastern Evening News, 11 February 1978

WHAT IS PRAYER?

Prayer is asking for things. Very true. This is indeed the basic meaning. 'I pray you do this' means 'I beg you', 'I beseech you'.

What may we ask for? We might ask for a bicycle or a pair of jeans or a box of chocolates: all good things at the right time. And Jesus tells us that we should ask God our Father for the simplest things we need. 'Give us today our daily bread.'

But, as we grow we shall see other things as important. We may ask God to increase our faith or to deepen our love, or to help us overcome some fault. And as we grow further we may come to ask for the greatest gift of all. Julian's prayer was: 'God, of your goodness, give me yourself, for only in you I have all.'

Our prayer is the exposure of the soul to God. Expose your injured arm to the doctor and he can work on it. Expose your spirit to God and he can work on it. Our problem nowadays is that we allow our minds to be worked on through study and our bodies through exercise, but too often not our spirits. We are all like three legged stools. The legs are called body, mind and spirit. For millions today the leg marked spirit is very feeble. And in a moment of crisis it is not just the leg that will collapse but the whole stool.

Or a definition I would like to leave with you. Prayer is a holding on to God until we move into the knowledge that we are being held. As we grow older our prayer will more and more take the form of a trustful resting in God.

I want to give you a picture. You will see the meaning later. You are in the kitchen and you turn on the tap. You might say that now all the water you could ever possibly want has become available to you. But alas you only have a cup. And that is all you can collect. Your friend beside you has a bucket so she can collect much more. And perhaps someone else has only a thimble and can take away hardly any at all.

When we go to prayer we draw on the immensity of God's love. The reservoir is huge but it's finite. God's love is infinite, inexhaustible. But perhaps I'm a cup and I can't hold much; or a bucket and I can hold more; or maybe I'm only a thimble.

It is through prayer, through breathing in the love of God that the spirit grows so that thimbles become cups, and cups become buckets, and buckets become baths, and for the saints baths become lakes.

How shall we pray? It depends where we are. But I suggest for most of us we take a New Testament and put ourselves into God's hands and read some verses from one of the gospels. Then think for a few moments what this has to say to you, some message on personal living perhaps. Suppose that takes five minutes or longer. Then for two minutes (for some it will be more) sit quite still in the way I am going to show you in a moment and allow God's

Holy Spirit to breathe his life into you.

Talk given to school children when, in the early 1990s, at their request, he blessed a prayer room at their school in Norfolk

THE BEST IS YET TO BE ... AWARENESS IN LOVE

'Please God, say hello to grandad who died last week.' Of all the intercession slips slotted into the prayer board at St Julian's Church, this one, written in disjointed childish letters, remains my favourite. Around it were prayers for sick people, for the lonely and depressed, for marriages moving towards the rocks, for parish and world needs. Most requests run on conventional lines, but occasionally there is something unusual. *'Please pray that my new shoes may stop pinching'* provided another refreshing break, and the memory has remained through the years.

Recently another prayer caught my attention. *'Pray for Mary* (as we will call her) *in old age who now feels she is of no use*

to anybody.' What lies behind a request like that? We may not have seen it on any list, but we all know of people who, after a lifetime of strenuous activity, find old age dull and pointless and believe there is nothing left to live for.

Mary (I am not speculating) was once a nurse in a general hospital. Many passed through her capable hands for relief in their sickness, thanking her, perhaps too as parents, for the care of their children. She had the challenge and fulfilment of sharing in a splendid team, the fascination of keeping abreast with modern techniques and medicines, the happiness of watching the sick recover. Now, forty years on, with failing eyesight and stiffening limbs, living mostly within the confines of her little house, largely dependent on those who choose to visit her, life has lost its sparkle and she finds herself depressed and confused. That it should ever have come to this! So useless now! What has gone wrong?

Mary has made the mistake – in some measure we all make it – of unconsciously identifying herself with her work. We assume this in her case because work stands for usefulness, and it is her present uselessness which bothers her. But you can, of course, identify yourself with much else besides – your standing in society, your style of dress, your way of speech, your possessions. It should be noticed that it is Mary's unconscious identification which is harmful. Conscious identification, as for the actor on the stage, who is today the hero and tomorrow the villain, is not damaging.

And Mary has neglected to identify herself with Mary, with the totally unique self which God had made and which she takes with her wherever she goes.

In her time she has been cast to play many roles, yet Mary herself is none of these, nor ever was. These are but the externals, changing their forms as the years go by, whereas Mary herself lies behind and beyond them all. Now in old age with so many of the trappings (a good word as so often they trap us) stripped away, she is perhaps being offered the chance as never before of discovering her true identity in God. This is growth, progress. She ought to be glad and not worried. It is regress, no doubt, as the world sees it, for Mary no longer counts as she once did, but in God's scale it is preparation, or the offer of preparation, for the enlarged perspectives that lie beyond this present life.

This is, after all, the only philosophy that can make sense to a Christian. For what in fact is Mary saying is that God made her and all men and women on the principle that we grow in usefulness for fifty or sixty years, after which a decline sets in whereby we become steadily of less and less use to God and one another? What a compliment to the architect who designed us as creatures for eternity!

Some years ago there lived in Norwich a young woman who, it seemed to me, was about as helpless as any living person could be. She had loved life and gaiety and friendship before sickness struck her down, and now with extraordinary courage faced her closing years. The one thing which seemed possible for her was to blow signals down a tube and this, with the help of the marvels of science, enabled her to switch lights on and off, and to lock and unlock doors, and even to operate the keys of a typewriter.

As she lay in bed almost unable to make herself understood she beamed contentment and joy: I recall the keen delight she took in passages of Julian's *Revelations* read to her. No one could have been more 'useless' than C, and yet it may be no one built up more fortitude and hope in the people around her. She had most truly found herself in God.

PICKING UP STRAWS FOR LOVE

C's opportunity is ours as we grow older. What matters is not the greatness of the work, but the love with which it is done. Brother Lawrence of the Resurrection, the author of the spiritual classic *The Practice of the Presence of God*, tells us three times in the course of a few pages how if we could but pick up a straw from the ground solely for the love of God, all perfection would lie in the act. Such a stupendous task, must of course, always lie beyond us; but we can move towards it, knowing that God looks for no more than what is within our power to do.

But perhaps you can no longer stoop so far as to pick up a straw.

So why not instead pick up your rosary, or a necklace would do, and pass the beads slowly through your fingers as an expression of your desire for God, putting into each movement such devotion and attention as is given you, allowing yourself gently to be aware of the touch on your fingertips, and letting God do the rest while your heart lies open to him? That is not the traditional way of saying the rosary, but it can be a very good way of moving into the contemplative silence before God which he wants you, with all of us, to enjoy.

Or you may prefer to find some short form of words to recite on each bead, a verse from the psalms perhaps, repeating it with such love and devotion as you may, until you have exhausted its meaning and the flavour has entered your soul. Or if you prefer to learn the traditional way – though perhaps you know it – find someone or some book which can help you. The practice will see you through many a lonely period and help to stabilise your heart in God.

Or if that is not your way, why not simply look around you with awareness, at the flowers in your room, upon a crucifix or icon or picture, or through the window to the trees and the sky. Awareness in love is here the secret, not concentration which blocks out everything else, but awareness which leaves you open to receive what God would have you find at this time.

Not that you can do any of these things all the time. But one or other may help to make a framework for the day, and leave an essence which will work its way into your relationships and indeed into all that you are able to do. Perhaps I have got you a bit wrong: you may have an interest or hobby you can pursue, or be able to get out sometimes and meet others.

What you need to be assured of is this: every action done in love, however insignificant it may seem, helps someone, somehow, somewhere, at some time. If you can make that an article of faith, and the great men and women of every major religion will assure you that you may, then you need never be at a loss for something useful to do.

I recall a letter from Archbishop Michael Ramsey in his retirement in which he spoke of 'uselessness' as opening the way for being truly useful in the service of God. The paradox is well worth pondering. Every contemplative will at once know what is meant, and the writer would have you know (for he was firm on this) that God desires for you the contemplative dimension in prayer, as for all who are seriously responding to him.

As a stone dropped into a pond sends ripples to each bank, so the healing power of love radiates from the still centre within to all creation. Your life may still be a help to many, and you too will be prepared, as in no other way, for the fuller vision of himself which God has for you, as for us all.

Article for *Christian* magazine,
July/August 1989

Peace Peace Peace

In 1981 Mother Teresa announced her Prayer for Peace asking that it be used around the world for one minute daily (either vocally or meditatively) at noon local time. A chain of prayer would thus be set up, activated at each of the twenty-four hours of the day. Clearly those who could not use the prayer at noon might do so at any other time.

> Lead me from death to life,
> From falsehood to truth.
> Lead me from despair to hope,
> From fear to trust.
> Lead me from hate to love,
> From war to peace.
> Let peace fill our heart, our world, our universe.
> Peace, Peace, Peace.

It will be noticed that the threefold peace is presented only after we have been led to reflect upon the things which make for peace. Also that Mother Teresa presents peace as beginning, not with the world, but with oneself: 'Lead me...' she writes. God's peace begins in the heart, extends to the home, so to the local community, the nation and the world. What if millions in every country used it vocally or meditatively daily as Mother Teresa asked!

But Mother Teresa was an apostle of silence and it may well be that of many she would have asked more. 'We need silence', she wrote, 'to be able to touch souls. God is a friend of silence.' Silence takes us to the heart of intercession. An intention before prayer is all that is needed. The pattern is unchanged. So far as we are enabled, thoughts and imaginations are released to fall unreflectingly into the arms of God. If they float around us that does not invalidate our prayer so long as we do not voluntarily attend to them. It is the desire for God that matters. He works. He knows. He understands.

The prayer is adapted from the Hindu scriptures and is suited to people of all faiths, indeed to every person of goodwill. Many feel helpless in our troubled times but the influence of faithful prayer is incalculable. And, like mercy, it is 'twice bless'd'; it blesses him that gives and him that takes.

A leaflet produced and distributed
by Robert Llewelyn

THE FRUITS OF PRAYER

THOUGHTS FROM *PRAYER AND CONTEMPLATION*

... And now our prayer time is over. What is it we have been doing? Well, in a sense, we have been taking a holiday, and if that sounds an odd way of putting it, remember that holidays often include doing hard and challenging things, like climbing mountains, or exploring unknown country. But this has been the best sort of holiday, for not only have we 'got away from it all' – which is essential on any holiday – but we have been in touch with the fount of all life and so have found *re*-creation of mind, body and spirit. We know how important it is to get away from our work from time to time, not to neglect it, but in order to see it in the perspective of eternity. And so we return to our work as before, and yet, not quite as before, for in this prayer the Holy Spirit has been active in the depths of our being, cleansing and purging us, healing and unifying the various sides of our nature. As a result we bring to our work a deeper integrity, a clearer perception of the real needs of those around us and – having come to grips with these things within ourselves – a fuller understanding of the fears and tensions which threaten to overwhelm others. Above all we bring a love disciplined and made strong through an ever-deeper union with God himself.

... I find it much easier to understand the man who denies absolutely the existence of God than the man who, believing in the God and Father of our Lord Jesus Christ, makes him deny us any active co-operation with him in the realm of prayer. That prayer *does* effect new things – that certain events which would not otherwise have happened do happen as a result of prayer being offered – Christians must surely believe beyond doubt. Yet, as we have seen, we need to balance this insight with another. We do not go to prayer that we may use God but that he may use us. We trust him to use our prayer as he wills in the extension of his blessing, and we trust him further to make us, through the discipline and training of prayer, more effective instruments of his will. One result of prayer will be to make us more fit to receive aright the good things, spiritual and material, which God wants to give. And prayer for one another will build us up into a fellowship of love, the deepest of all blessings, from which much else will flow.

... only the Holy Spirit can teach us how to pray. We can of course find help and direction from books and from people, but in the end, prayer is the work of the Holy Spirit within us and he alone is the teacher. The Spirit, says St Paul, comes to the aid of our weakness. We do not even know how we ought to pray, but 'the Spirit himself makes intercession for us with groanings that cannot be uttered'. Here perhaps we are coming close to a definition of contemplative prayer – 'Groanings which cannot be uttered', 'sighs too deep for words', or, in the paraphrase supplied by one of the commentaries, 'inexpressible longings which God alone understands'. Contemplation is indeed a gift, the gift of the Spirit which only he can impart and only he can develop within us. It should be sought by waiting rather than by effort, gently, and with a patience that abides in God's time rather than urging our own desires.

… We are perhaps accustomed to think of contemplative prayer as belonging to those times when we kneel or sit or stand in silence in the presence of God. Certainly the heart's silence is of the essence of such prayer, but this does not necessarily mean the absence of words, and there will be many times when the recitation of the divine office or some other form of vocal prayer, such as the rosary, will reveal themselves as contemplative in nature.

… *Love is my meaning*. These words, adapted from Mother Julian, hold the key to all that has been said and all that can still be said, whatever the nature of our calling in prayer. No method of prayer can of itself be valid apart from the dimension of love. In prayer love is expressed and deepened, and yet more, it is re-fashioned as … it takes its form from the wisdom and perfection of God."

Some thoughts from
Prayer and Contemplation
(SLG Press, 1975)

Insights from Over the Years

… I have found it helpful to see vocal prayer like this. See the words as the banks of a river and the prayer, that is to say the inclination of the heart to God, as the river itself. The banks are very important because they keep the river deep, and they keep it flowing. But it is the river which really matters. So, too, it is the uniting of the heart with God in prayer which really matters; the words simply help to that end. When the river reaches the sea the banks are no longer needed and drop away, and we are left in the silence in the ocean of God's love.

… Allow the prayer to do its own work. At first you must pray. But later you may allow yourself *to be prayed*. At the beginning of prayer our consciousness is in holding on to God. Later we are enabled to rest in the knowledge that he is holding on to us. And that is the better part of prayer.

From *Memories and* Reflections,
(Darton, Longman and Todd, 1998)

WE MUST LEARN TO BE

… If you want to learn to pray, you must understand that being is more important than doing.

It is not that doing is unimportant. It is rather that right doing springs from right being.

Much of our doing does not spring from our being. Instead of expressing our being our doing often disguises it.

When our being is firmly rooted in Christ our doing will no longer mask our being. It will be as good fruit springing from a good tree rooted in soil which is good.

God is the ground of our being. Through prayer we become rooted in him who is our ground.

When we are rightly grounded, our whole nature – bodily, mental and spiritual

– will be integrated or made whole. Our experience of discord will be replaced by one of harmony.

From *A Doorway to Silence*
(Darton, Longman and Todd, 1986)